My Catholic Lent an Activity Book

Reproducible Sheets for Home and School

Written and Illustrated by Jennifer Galvin

Paulist Press
New York/Mahwah, N.J.

For Mark, Matthew, Alex, and Becca who love me unconditionally—even when I'm drawing.

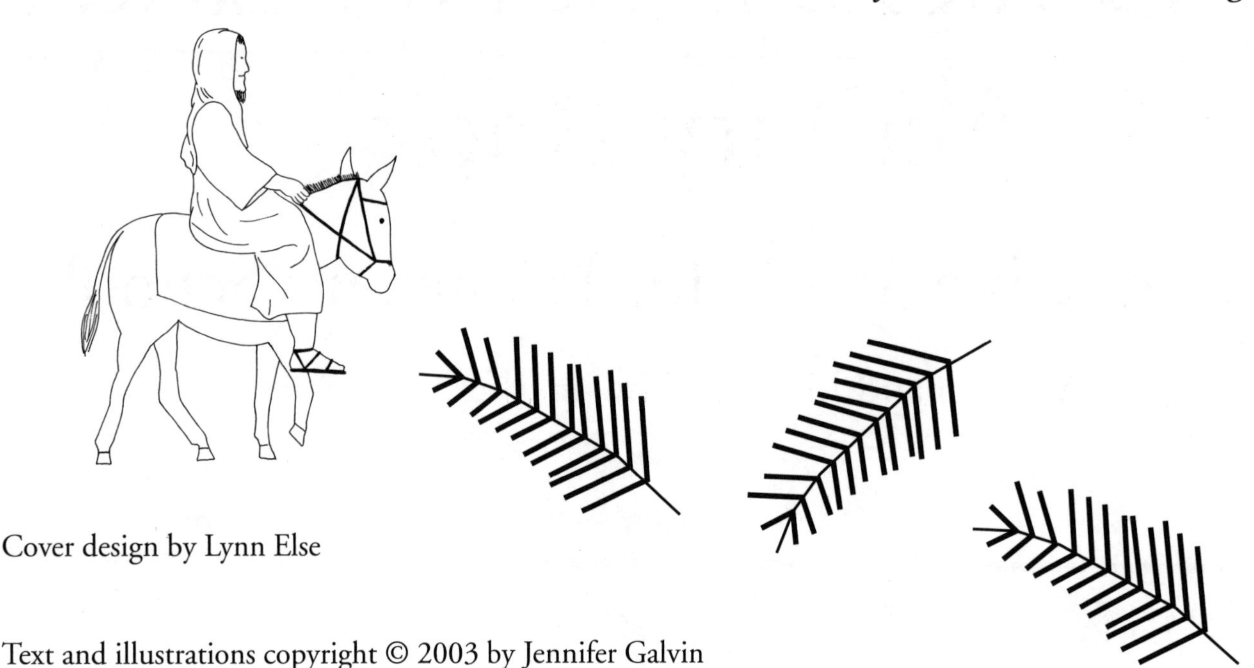

Cover design by Lynn Else

ISBN: 0-8091-6706-9

Published by Paulist Press
997 Macarthur Boulevard
Mahwah, New Jersey 07430

www.paulistpress.com

Printed and bound in the United States of America
by McNaughton & Gunn, Inc.
Saline, MI
12/2017

Act of Contrition

Lent is a time to remember everything that happened to Jesus before his crucifixion and resurrection. By remembering, we prepare for the church's most important celebration—Easter. Another way to prepare ourselves is to show God through prayer that we're sorry for our sins. Find all of the words in the Act of Contrition that are in **bold** print.

```
N W E I J N G O D I N M P W N V
W T G C X B N M P R T H J D C H
Y R O N C M M E R C Y P E B N E
P W O B N H X C P T R N C V B A
P Y D N C V O T Y P N R T V B R
F J N V G P W O N I Y H W P H T
A B V P W R T Y S C X P T H X M
I N T E N D G H M I P Z X N O P
L C V T Y P Z B N Y N P M L K M
I B L E A D S N A V C G H O B Y
N V H Y T R Y B V P Y R C V G Y
G H R C X R T Y O N S W P E N J
B A X H R Y T N I Y H P B V Z E
V M C O P D I E D N M E V C X S
N E S Y P R W X C V M L L P R U
P N Y P E N A N C E G T B P X S
```

My **God**, I am **sorry** for my sins with all my **heart.** In **choosing** to do **wrong** and **failing** to do **good,** I have **sinned** against you **whom** I should **love** above all things. I firmly **intend,** with your **help,** to do **penance,** to sin no more, and to **avoid** whatever **leads** me to sin.

Our Savior **Jesus** Christ suffered and **died** for us. In his name, my God, have **mercy. Amen.**

Ash Wednesday

Ash Wednesday is the first day of the Lenten season, the season leading up to Easter. On Ash Wednesday we remember that we came from dust and would return to dust forever if Jesus had not died for our sins.

Across

1. Before the ashes are brought to the Ash Wednesday Mass, they have been sprinkled with _ _ _ _ water and are scented with incense.
4. Ashes remind us of our _ _ _ _ for redemption.
6. On Ash Wednesday, the _ _ _ _ _ _ puts ashes on our heads.
7. The ashes are _ _ _ _ _ _ _ _ with four prayers.
9. Ashes remind us of our original _ _ _.

Down

2. Ash Wednesday is the first day of _ _ _ _.
3. The priest puts the ashes on our heads in the shape of a _ _ _ _ _.
5. The ashes are made from _ _ _ _ leaves from last year's Palm Sunday.
8. When the ashes are placed on our heads, the priest says, "You are dust, and to _ _ _ _ you shall return." (Genesis 3:19)

Lent Coloring Page

Some people make sacrifices during Lent. For example, they give up their favorite candy or TV show, or they say extra prayers. Other people do good deeds. Elizabeth is helping her neighbor plant a flower garden.
What will *you* do this Lent?

Mary Anoints Jesus

"Mary took a pound of costly perfume made of pure nard, anointed Jesus' feet, and wiped them with her hair." (John 12:3) Find all twelve things that are different in the second picture.

Holy Week

Match each Holy Week term with its definition.

Holy Week	On this day we remember how the people of Jerusalem welcomed Jesus as the Messiah, waving palm branches and praising his name.
Palm Sunday	On this day we remember the time that Jesus spent in the tomb.
Triduum	Jesus celebrated a last supper with his apostles on this day. He gave them and all of us the gift of himself in the Eucharist.
Holy Thursday	Jesus suffered and died for us on the cross on this day.
Good Friday	The end of Lent. During this week, we remember what happened to Jesus before his resurrection.
Holy Saturday	This takes place on Holy Saturday night. Christ has defeated death and won for us life in heaven. We wait for his return!
Easter Vigil	This Latin word means three days. It is the special name we give to Holy Thursday, Good Friday, and Holy Saturday—the end of Holy Week.

Palm Sunday

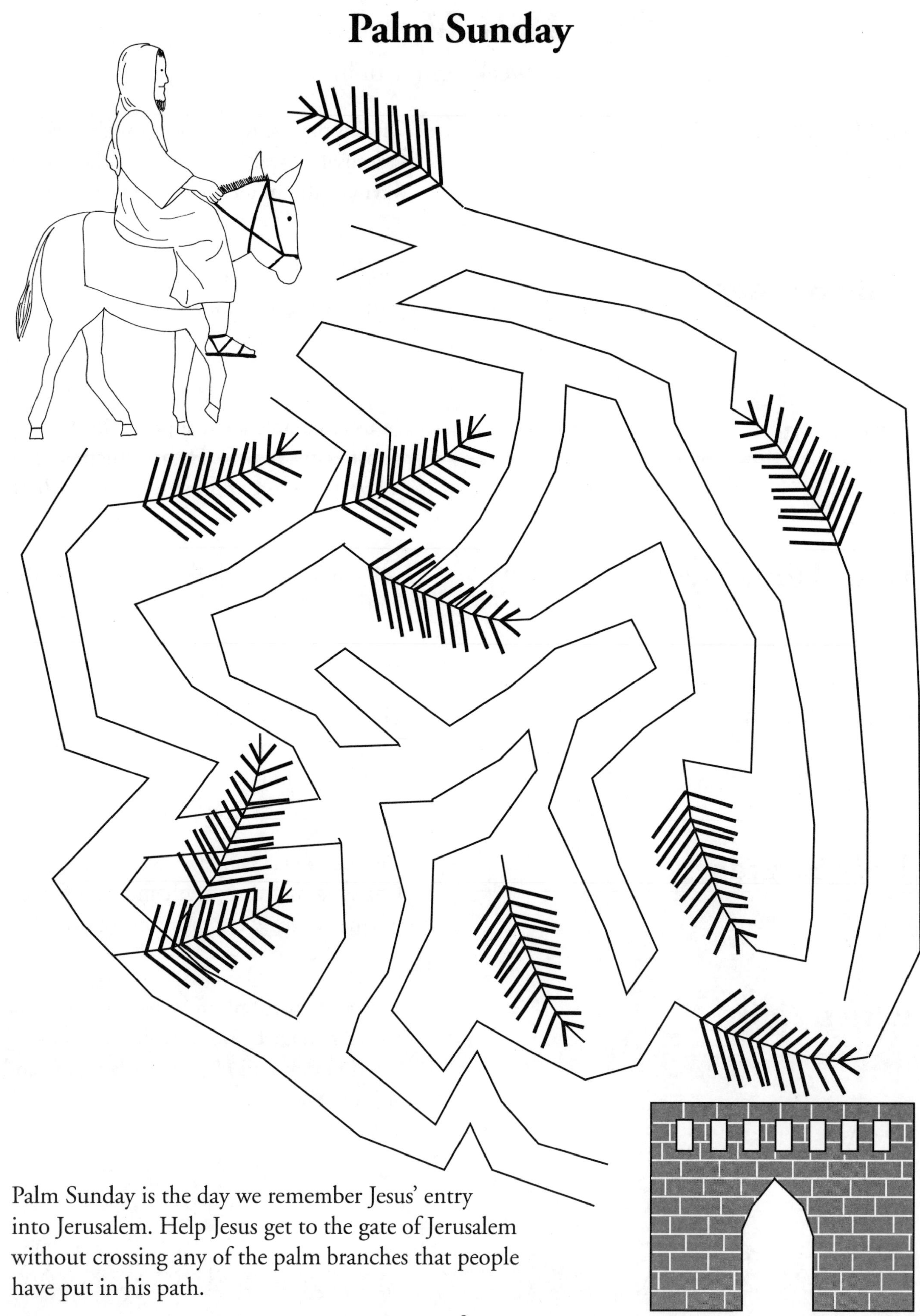

Palm Sunday is the day we remember Jesus' entry into Jerusalem. Help Jesus get to the gate of Jerusalem without crossing any of the palm branches that people have put in his path.

Washing of the Feet

On the night of the Last Supper, Jesus washed the disciples' feet. If Jesus, their Lord, washed their feet, they then should wash one another's feet. This meant they should be of service to each other.

On Holy Thursday, the priest washes the feet of people from the parish. This helps us remember Jesus' act and that we, too, should serve each other. Find all thirteen things that don't belong in this picture.

Jesus Gives Us Himself

Connect the dots to see how Jesus gave himself to us at the Last Supper. Through these, he is truly present to us at Mass, body and blood, through the mystery of the Eucharist.

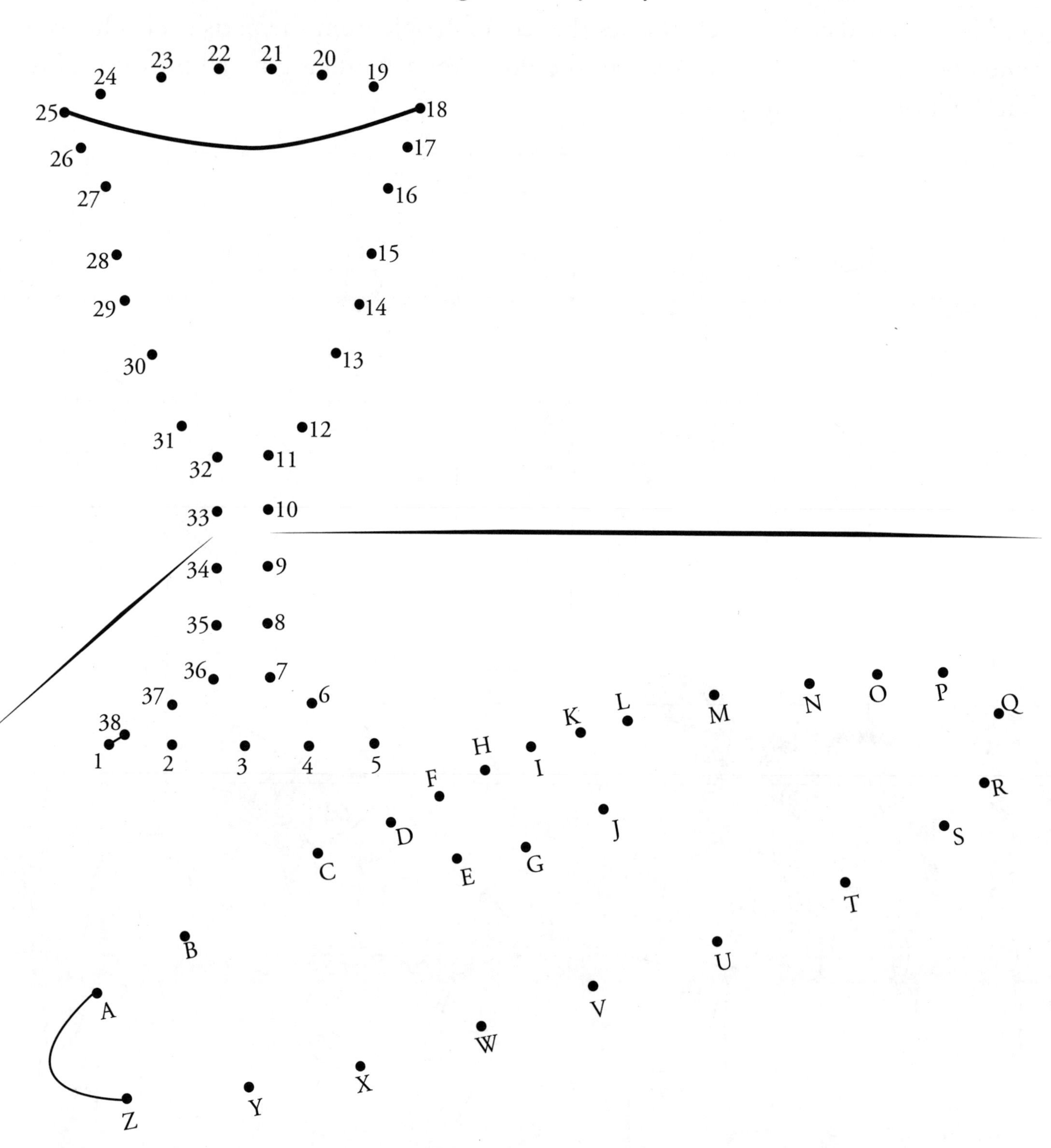

Jesus is present to us through b _ _ _ _ and w _ _ _.

Sort out the Silver

Who betrayed Jesus for thirty pieces of silver?

To find out, follow the line from each box to a piece of silver.

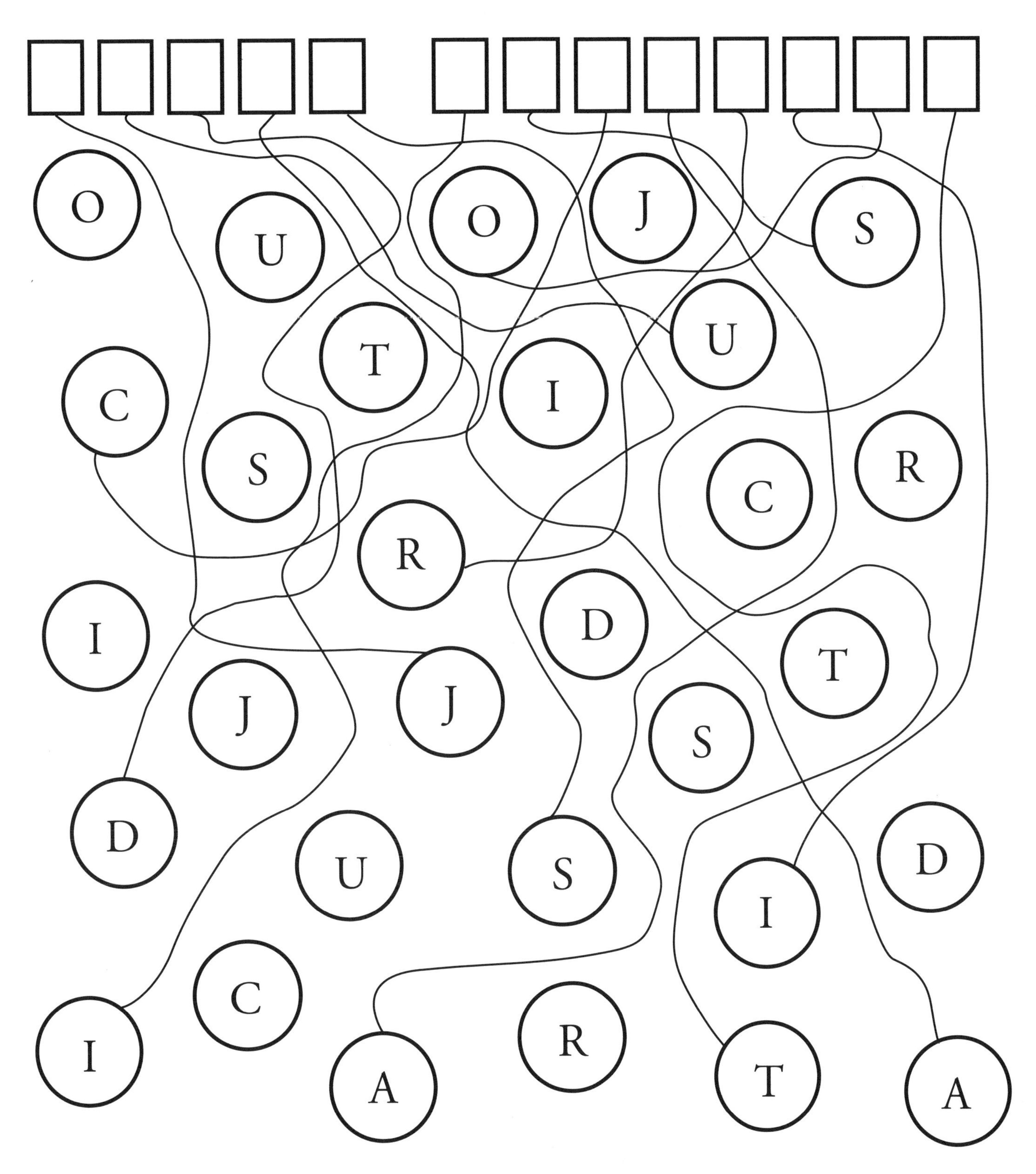

Jesus before Pilate

After the chief priests arrested Jesus, they gave him a trial before the Sanhedrin. The Sanhedrin was the Jewish Supreme Court. Since by Jewish law the Sanhedrin could not condemn Jesus to death, the high priests turned him over to Pilate, the Roman governor. Pilate had the power to crucify Jesus. Unscramble the words to learn what happened.

1. Pilate asked _ _ _ _ _,"Are you the King of the Jews?" USSEJ

2. Jesus answered, "_ _ _ say so." OUY

3. Jesus would not answer the accusations made by the chief _ _ _ _ _ _ _ _. SPTSREI

4. Pilate offered to set Jesus _ _ _ _. EREF

5. The chief priests got the people to ask for _ _ _ _ _ _ _ _ _. BBBAAARS

6. Pilate feared the crowd would _ _ _ _ if he didn't free the prisoner the people wanted. TROI

7. The people asked for Jesus to be _ _ _ _ _ _ _ _ _ _ _. RDCCFIIUE

8. Pilate _ _ _ _ _ _ his hands of Jesus' innocent blood. DWSHAE

9. Pilate then had Jesus _ _ _ _ _ _ _ _ _. CSDEOUGR

10. After this, Pilate turned Jesus over to the _ _ _ _ _ _ to be crucified. DRGUSA

Anima Christi

The Anima Christi, or Soul of Christ, was written in Latin over six hundred years ago. It is so old that no one remembers who wrote it. This prayer may be said any time. It is often said after receiving holy communion or while praying before the Blessed Sacrament. You can also pray this on Good Friday. Find all of the words in the Anima Christi that are in **bold** print.

```
S Y P R O T E C T B N B Z B N
O T R H G B N M T Y V B O V C
U W A T G H M S Z S J I C D D
L B I B N M I A P T G H P W Y
L B S P Z R B V R R P T R M N
H J E T H T N E E E P W V B P
W R B C P W F R D N S D P C A
A W Z P S A X F Y G J E S U S
S A I N T S S T X T B H M N S
Y P W R V H I S S H P R T Y I
B V C G H N R D P E X S L M O
L O V E R H N C V N C P T Y N
O T Y E B U W S X N M A P T I
O C T B O Z S W R T P L L H Y
D E N W L W A T E R N H O L Y
```

Soul of **Christ**, make me **holy**. **Body** of Christ, **save** me. **Blood** of Christ, fill me with **love**. **Water** from Christ's side, **wash** me. **Passion** of Christ, **strengthen** me. Oh good **Jesus**, hear me. Within your **wounds**, hide me. Never let me be parted from you. From the evil enemy, **protect** me. At the hour of my death, **call** me, and tell me to come to you, that with your **saints** I may **praise** you through all **eternity**. Amen.

The Crucifixion

Good Friday is the day we remember Jesus' crucifixion. Do this crossword to see how much you remember about the crucifixion. Fill in what you know, then reread Matthew 27:32–61 if you need help.

Across

2. _ _ _ _ _ _ _ of Arimathea asked Pilate for Jesus' body.
4. Jesus had to carry his own _ _ _ _ _.
6. The _ _ _ _ _ _ _ _ _ cast lots to divide Jesus' clothing.
8. When Jesus died, the _ _ _ _ _ _ _ in the temple was torn in two.

Down

1. _ _ _ other people were crucified with Jesus, one on each side of him.
2. The chief priests and other people mocked _ _ _ _ _ while he was on the cross, saying he should be able to save himself.
3. Joseph wrapped Jesus in a linen cloth and laid him in the _ _ _ _.
5. The inscription above Jesus read, "This is the _ _ _ _ of the Jews."
7. _ _ _ _ _ helped Jesus carry his cross.

Saint Veronica

Crack the code to find the answer to the question below. First do the addition problems. Then fill in the blanks with the letter that matches the number under the blank.

A:__=1+1	H:__=5+5	O:__=5+4	V:__=12+11
B:__=20+6	I:__=2+2	P:__=10+9	W:__=9+9
C:__=4+4	J:__=7+7	Q:__=23+2	X:__=10+7
D:__=2+5	K:__=20+4	R:__=2+3	Y:__=10+10
E:__=1+0	L:__=9+6	S:__=3+3	Z:__=10+11
F:__=8+5	M:__=8+8	T:__=2+1	
G:__=6+6	N:__=6+5	U:__=11+11	

As Jesus carried his cross to Golgotha, his face became bloody and sweaty.
St. Veronica saw this and wiped his face for him.
What happened to St. Veronica's cloth when she wiped Jesus' face?

__ __   __ __ __ __ __   __ __
2 11   4 16 2 12 1   9 13

__ __ __ __ __   __ __ __ __ __ __ __ __
14 1 6 22 6   2 19 19 1 2 5 1 7

__ __   __ __ __   __ __ __ __ __.
9 11   10 1 5   8 15 9 3 10

The Stations of the Cross

In the Stations of the Cross, we remember how Jesus suffered and died for us. There are fourteen stations. First, write the name of the stations in order. The pictures will give you clues. To pray the Stations of the Cross, begin each station with this prayer:

We adore thee, O Christ, and we bless you,
because by your holy cross you have redeemed the world.

Look at the station and think about what it means. Pray an Our Father, a Hail Mary, and a Glory Be. Then look at the next station and say the prayer again.

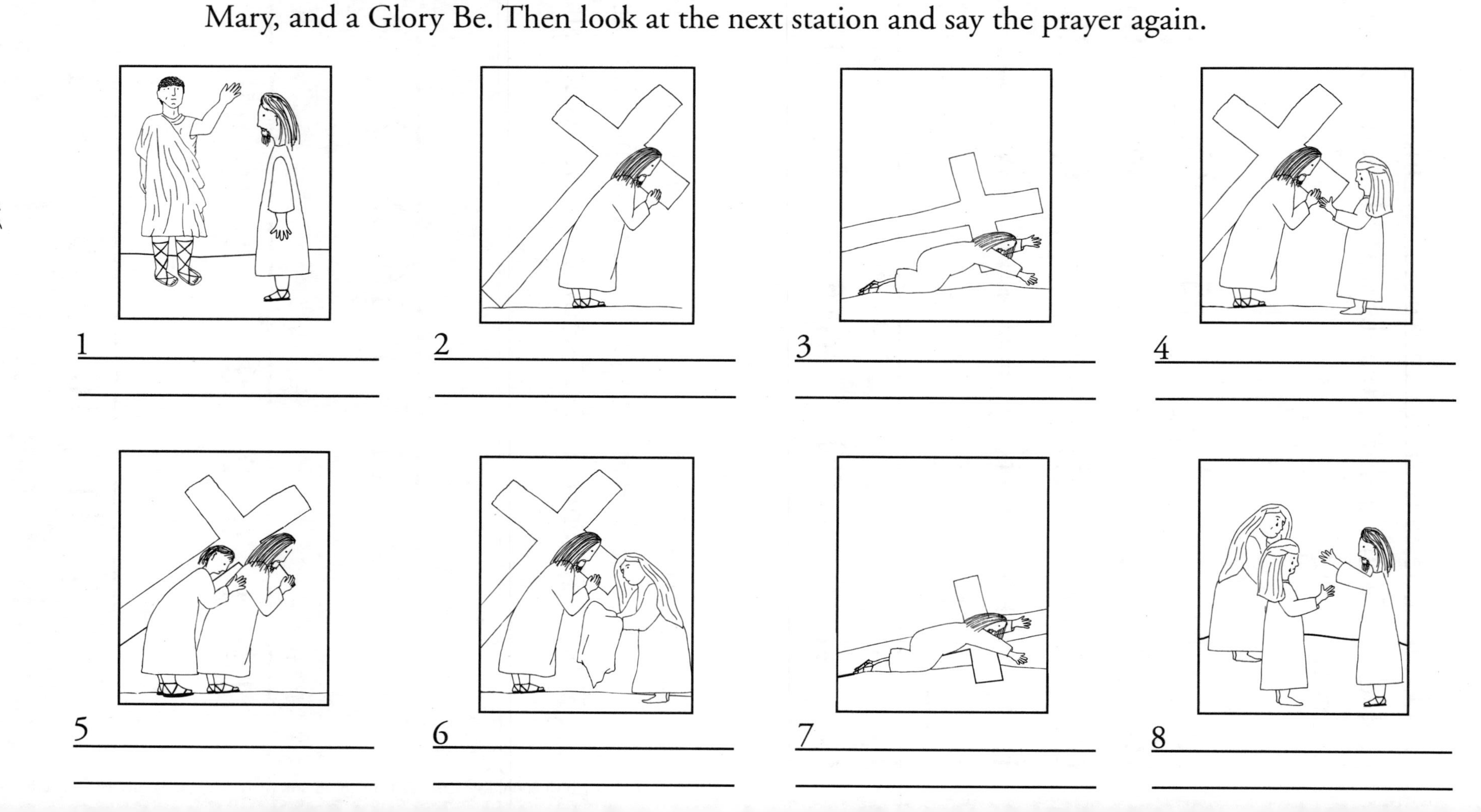

1 ______________________

2 ______________________

3 ______________________

4 ______________________

5 ______________________

6 ______________________

7 ______________________

8 ______________________

Jesus comforts the women of Jerusalem • Jesus is nailed to the cross • Jesus falls a third time

Jesus dies • Jesus is condemned to death • Veronica wipes Jesus' face

Jesus is laid in the tomb • Jesus falls a second time • Jesus is taken from the cross

Jesus is stripped of his clothes • Jesus takes up the cross

Jesus meets his mother • Jesus falls the first time • Simon of Cyrene helps Jesus carry the cross

Veneration of the Cross

Another way to remember Jesus' death on Good Friday is to venerate, or show respect to, the cross on which he died. Look at the picture to find out how we do this, write your answer below, then color the picture.

We show our respect for Jesus and the cross by _ _ _ _ _ _ _ the crucifix.

Color by Number

Color the picture, then answer the question below.

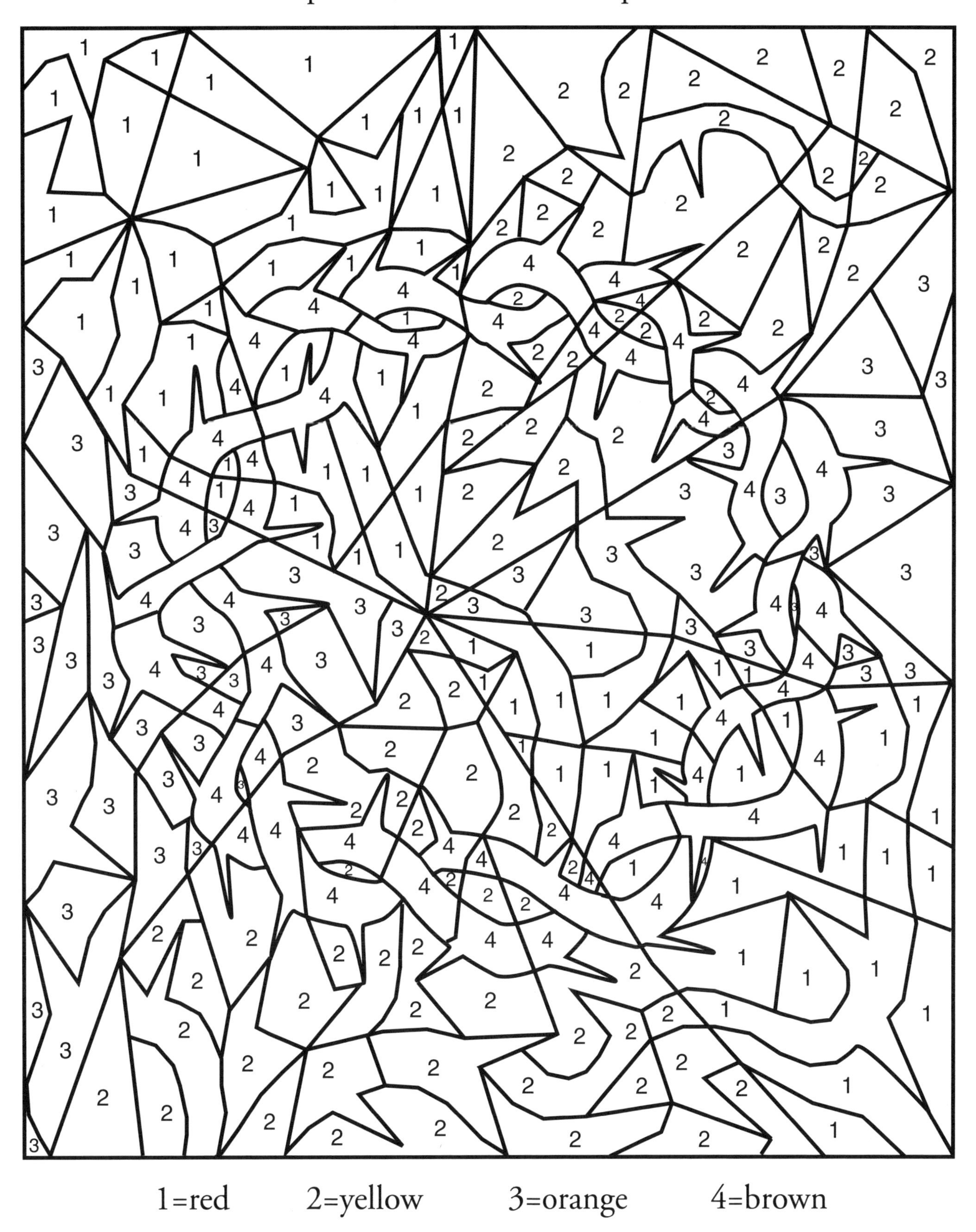

1=red 2=yellow 3=orange 4=brown

What did the soldiers put on Jesus' head? ____________________

The Easter Vigil

The risen Christ is the light of the world! As baptized Christians, we share in that light and in that life! Color by number to see how we remember this during the Easter Vigil.

1=red 2=yellow 3=brown 4=your skin color

5=blue 6=orange 7=white

Easter Sunday

Easter Sunday marks the end of Lent. On Easter Sunday we remember that Jesus conquered death. Easter Sunday is the first day of the Easter season, which lasts for fifty days.The last day of the Easter season is Pentecost.

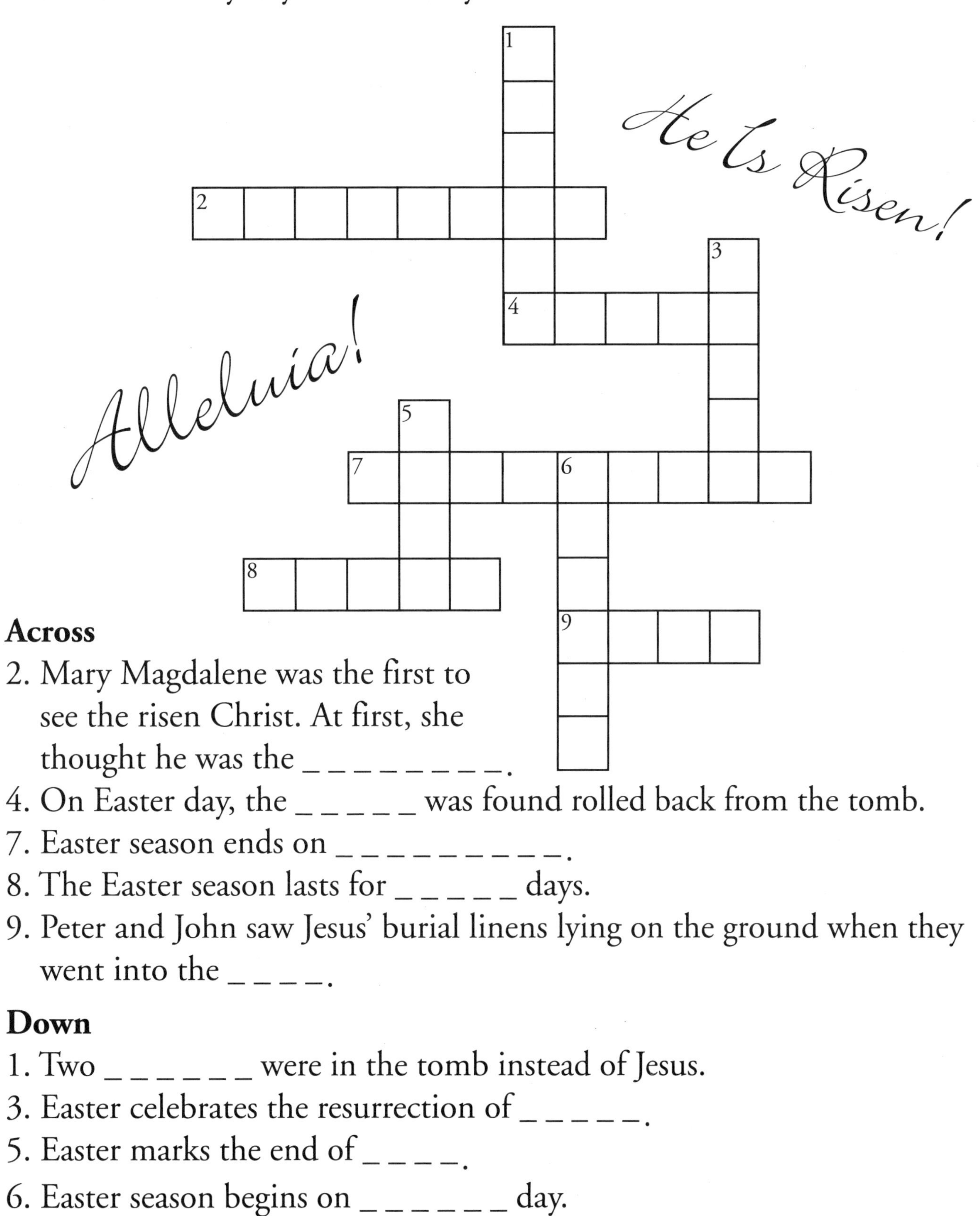

Across

2. Mary Magdalene was the first to see the risen Christ. At first, she thought he was the _ _ _ _ _ _ _ _ _.
4. On Easter day, the _ _ _ _ _ was found rolled back from the tomb.
7. Easter season ends on _ _ _ _ _ _ _ _ _ _.
8. The Easter season lasts for _ _ _ _ _ days.
9. Peter and John saw Jesus' burial linens lying on the ground when they went into the _ _ _ _.

Down

1. Two _ _ _ _ _ _ were in the tomb instead of Jesus.
3. Easter celebrates the resurrection of _ _ _ _ _.
5. Easter marks the end of _ _ _ _.
6. Easter season begins on _ _ _ _ _ _ day.

He Is Risen!

On Easter Sunday, we celebrate Jesus' rising from the dead to go to heaven to be with God, his Father.

Where are the angels? ______________________________.

Who used to be here? ______________________________.

What happened to him? ______________________________.

Mary Magdalene Sees Jesus

After Mary Magdalene saw the angels in the tomb, she turned around and thought she saw the gardener. When the man spoke, she recognized him as the risen Christ. Look at the two pictures of Mary Magdalene and Jesus. Find all 14 things that are different in the second picture, then color the pictures.

Easter Symbols

There are many symbols for the Easter season. These symbols all have to do with new life. They help us remember that Jesus rose from the dead to bring us a new life with God. Color the symbols. Then match each symbol to its definition.

Goes into a chrysalis as a caterpillar and emerges after several days as this.

Symbol of the risen Christ.

Looks a little like a stone, but when it cracks open, a new life comes out.

The Doubting Disciple

One disciple would not believe Jesus had risen. He said that before he would believe he needed to see and touch Jesus for himself. What was that disciple's name?

To find the answer, look at the symbols under each space below. Use the chart to find which letter goes in each space. Follow the first symbol across and the second symbol up to find each letter. Put the letter in the space.

	N	T	R	M
	H	B	O	C
	A	G	E	S

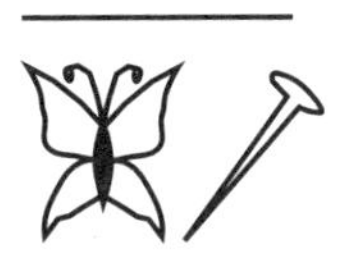

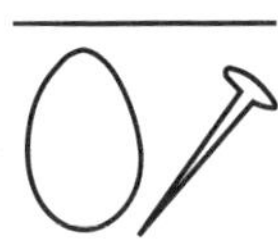
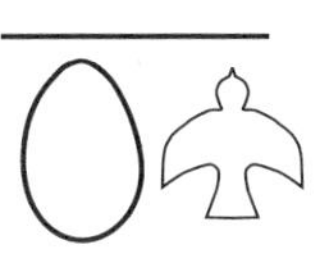

Emmaus

Two of Jesus' friends were walking to Emmaus. A third man joined them on the road. They asked him to join them for dinner. When he broke the bread and blessed it, they realized it was Jesus. Just then he disappeared. They hurried back to Jerusalem to tell the disciples. Help these men meet Jesus and then return to Jerusalem.

Coloring Page of the Ascension

"While he was blessing them, he withdrew from them and was carried up into heaven. And they worshiped him, and returned to Jerusalem with great joy; and they were continually in the temple blessing God." (Luke 24:51–53)

The Upper Room

Unscramble the letters to find out about the coming of the Holy Spirit.

1. Jesus first mentioned the _ _ _ _   _ _ _ _ _ _ to the disciples at the Last Supper in the upper room. YLHO   TRIISP

2. Jesus said _ _ _ would send the Holy Spirit in Jesus' name. DGO

3. The Holy Spirit would _ _ _ _ _ the disciples. HACET

4. The Holy Spirit would also _ _ _ _ _ _ the disciples of all Jesus taught them. DMRINE

5. After Jesus _ _ _ _ from the dead, he appeared to the disciples. OESR

6. Jesus showed the _ _ _ _ _ _ _ _ _ his hands and side. ELIISCPDS

7. Jesus said to the disciples, "_ _ _ _ _ be with you. As the Father has sent me, so I send you." (John 20:21) EAECP

8. Then Jesus _ _ _ _ _ _ _ _ on the disciples and gave them the Holy Spirit. TDEEHBRA

9. Jesus gave the disciples the Holy Spirit to be with them on _ _ _ _ _, since he would be up in heaven with God. THERA

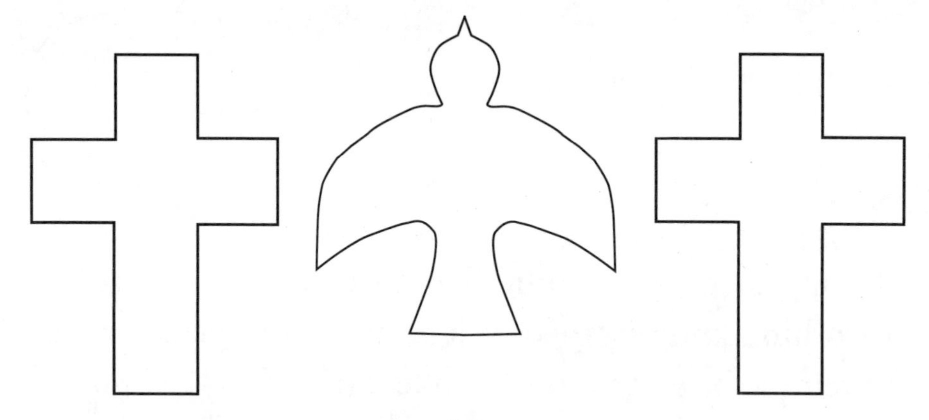

Prayer to the Holy Spirit

Jesus sent the Holy Spirit to be with us always while we wait for him to return. This is a prayer we use to ask the Holy Spirit for his guidance. Find all of the words in the prayer that are in **bold** print.

```
H K L N M S E N D T K N V C G
G O D V B P Q W C V B L X L F
J K L V R E N E W C U F L R I
X C G Y T R W Z B F G A P R L
V B N P S R T B H G H R H L L
P K R T Y P W T P S T W X V K
R I P R T K I W X S P I R I T
U N R T P A G R X B H F X C M
M D G H F P C Y I G D A H V T
G L V B N Y P R D T B C W X B
N E A R T H B C E R T E P R T
E A R T T H T L W A T F I R E
T R G R T G H O V V T P R W X
J V O C E A R V B N J E G P W
Y F V S T R A E H P M W D N X
```

Prayer to the Holy Spirit

Come, **Holy Spirit**,
fill the **hearts** of your **faithful**
and **kindle** in them
the **fire** of your **love**.
Send forth your **Spirit**,
and they **shall** be **created**.
And you shall **renew**
the **face** of the **earth**. Amen.

Gifts of the Holy Spirit

The Holy Spirit brings us seven special gifts. The gifts are *wisdom, understanding, counsel, fortitude, knowledge, piety,* and *fear of the Lord.* We will receive these gifts in confirmation. These gifts make the entire church stronger by helping each of us hear and follow God's word better. Below are the gifts with their letters scrambled up. Unscramble the letters to learn what each gift means.

1. _ _ _ _ of the Lord is the gift of being aware of God's presence among us. AERF

2. _ _ _ _ _ _ _ _ is the gift of judging correctly whether things are right or wrong. EOUSCLN

3. _ _ _ _ _ _ _ _ _ _ _ _ _ _ _ _ is the gift of seeing what is true in religion. GDSTUNNREADIN

4. _ _ _ _ _ _ _ _ _ _ _ is the gift of knowing clearly what to do to win heaven. OWEEGDKNL

5. _ _ _ _ _ _ _ is the gift of knowing and loving only those things that lead us to heaven. MSWDIO

6. _ _ _ _ _ _ is the gift of feeling deep respect and reverence for God. EIYPT

7. _ _ _ _ _ _ _ _ _ _ _ is the gift of being strong and brave when faced with problems or with temptations. IUTTDFEOR

Answers

Page 3

Page 4

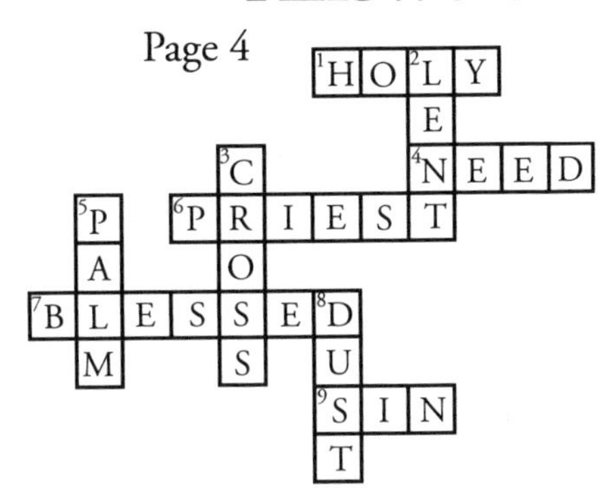

Page 6

Page 7

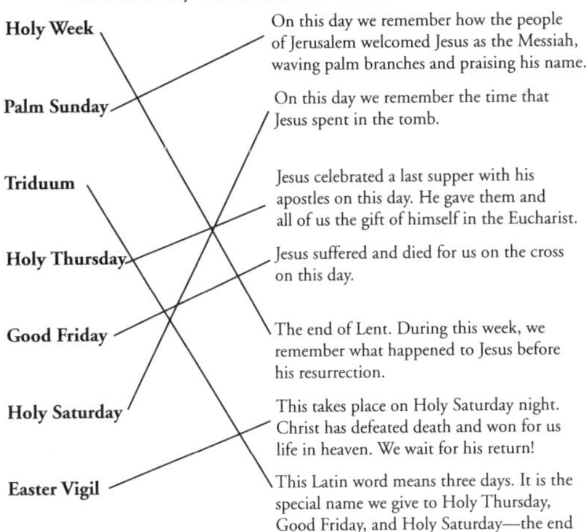

Page 8

Palm Sunday

Page 9

Page 10

Jesus is present to us through BREAD and WINE.

Page 11

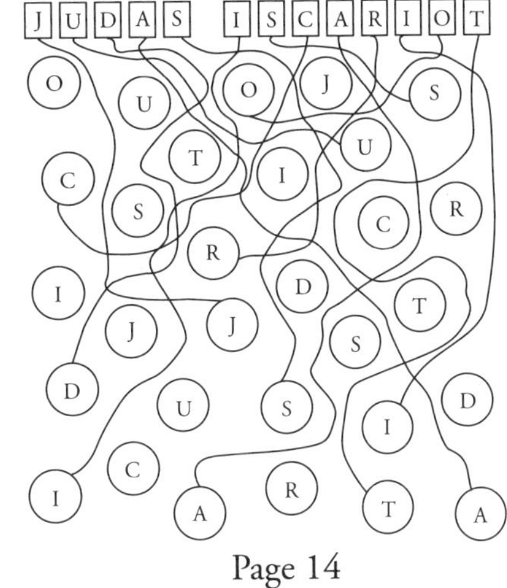

Page 12

1. Pilate asked JESUS, "Are you the King of the Jews?"
2. Jesus answered, "YOU say so."
3. Jesus would not answer the accusations made by the chief PRIESTS.
4. Pilate offered to set Jesus FREE.
5. The chief priests got the people to ask for BARABBAS.
6. Pilate feared the crowd would RIOT if he didn't free the prisoner the people wanted.
7. The people asked for Jesus to be CRUCIFIED.
8. Pilate WASHED his hands of Jesus' innocent blood.
9. Pilate then had Jesus SCOURGED.
10. After this, Pilate turned Jesus over to the GUARDS to be crucified.

Page 13

Page 14

1 TWO
2 JOSEPH
3 TOMB
4 CROSS
5 KING
6 SOLDIERS
7 SIMON
8 CURTAIN
JESUS

Page 15

A: 2 =1+1	H: 10 =5+5	O: 9 =5+4	V: 23 =12+11
B: 26 =20+6	I: 4 =2+2	P: 19 =10+9	W: 18 =9+9
C: 8 =4+4	J: 14 =7+7	Q: 25 =23+2	X: 17 =10+7
D: 7 =2+5	K: 24 =20+4	R: 5 =2+3	Y: 20 =10+10
E: 1 =1+0	L: 15 =9+6	S: 6 =3+3	Z: 21 =10+11
F: 13 =8+5	M: 16 =8+8	T: 3 =2+1	
G: 12 =6+6	N: 11 =6+5	U: 22 =11+11	

As Jesus carried his cross to Golgotha, his face became bloody and sweaty. St. Veronica saw this and wiped his face for him. What happened to St. Veronica's cloth when she wiped Jesus' face?

AN IMAGE OF
2 11 4 16 2 12 1 9 13

JESUS APPEARED
14 1 6 22 6 2 19 19 1 2 5 1 7

ON HER CLOTH.
9 11 10 1 5 8 15 9 3 10

Answers

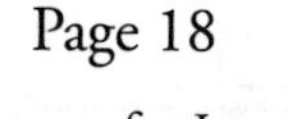

Pages 16-17

1. Jesus is condemned to death.
2. Jesus takes up the cross.
3. Jesus falls the first time.
4. Jesus meets his mother.
5. Simon of Cyrene helps Jesus carry the cross.
6. Veronica wipes Jesus' face.
7. Jesus falls a second time.
8. Jesus comforts the women of Jerusalem.
9. Jesus falls a third time.
10. Jesus is stripped of his clothes.
11. Jesus is nailed to the cross.
12. Jesus dies.
13. Jesus is taken from the cross.
14. Jesus is laid in the tomb.

Page 18

We show our respect for Jesus and the cross by KISSING the crucifix.

Page 19

What did the soldiers put on Jesus' head?
A crown of thorns.

Page 21

1 ANGEL
2 GARDENER
3 JESUS
4 STONE
5 LENT
6 EASTER
7 PENTECOST
8 FIFTY
9 TOMB

Page 23

Page 22

On Easter Sunday, we celebrate Jesus' rising from the dead to go to heaven to be with God, his Father.

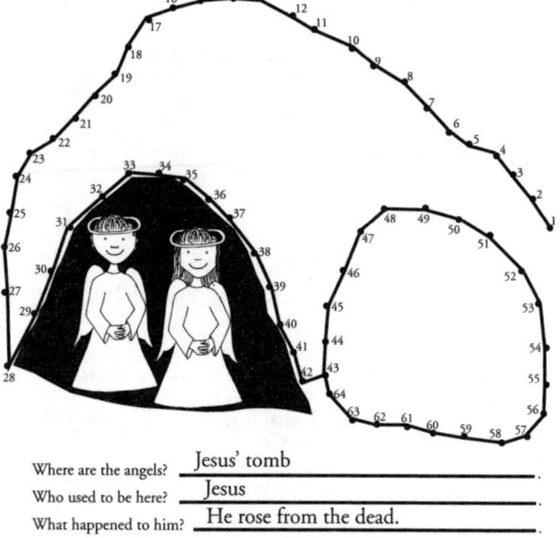

Where are the angels? Jesus' tomb
Who used to be here? Jesus
What happened to him? He rose from the dead.

Page 24

Goes into a chrysalis as a caterpillar and emerges after several days as this.
Symbol of the risen Christ.
Looks a little like a stone, but when it cracks open, a new life comes out.

Page 25

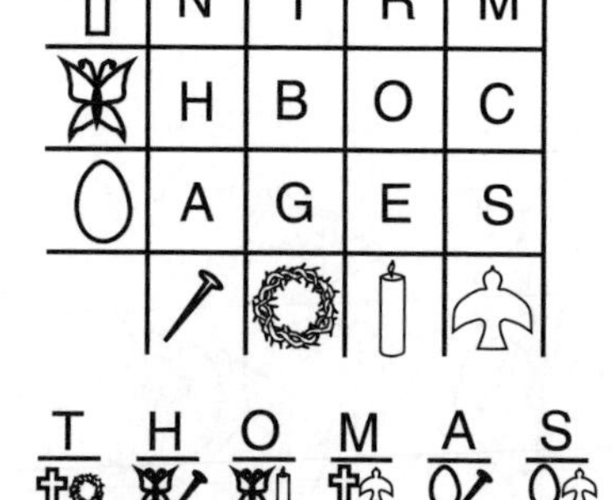

Page 26

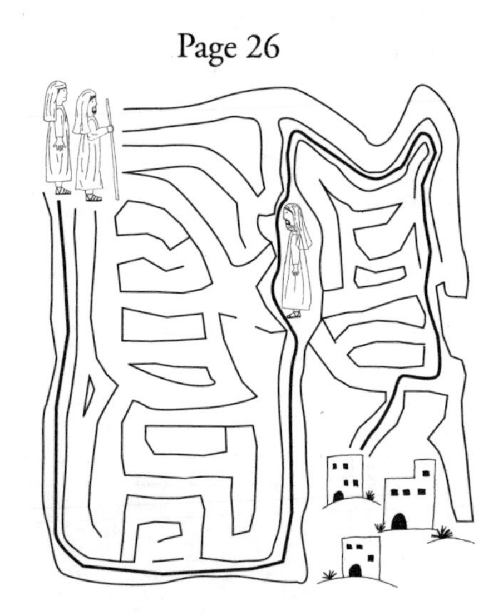

Page 28

1. Jesus first mentioned the HOLY SPIRIT to the disciples at the Last Supper in the upper room.
2. Jesus said GOD would send the Holy Spirit in Jesus' name.
3. The Holy Spirit would TEACH the disciples.
4. The Holy Spirit would also REMIND the disciples of all Jesus taught them.
5. After Jesus ROSE from the dead, he appeared to the disciples.
6. Jesus showed the DISCIPLES his hands and side.
7. Jesus said to the disciples, "PEACE be with you. As the Father has sent me, so I send you." (John 20:21)
8. Then Jesus BREATHED on the disciples and gave them the Holy Spirit.
9. Jesus gave the disciples the Holy Spirit to be with them on EARTH, since he would be up in heaven with God.

Page 29

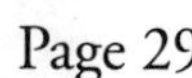
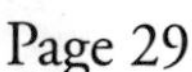

Page 30

1. FEAR of the Lord is the gift of being aware of God's presence among us.
2. COUNSEL is the gift of judging correctly whether things are right or wrong.
3. UNDERSTANDING is the gift of seeing what is true in religion.
4. KNOWLEDGE is the gift of knowing clearly what to do to win heaven.
5. WISDOM is the gift of knowing and loving only those things that lead us to heaven.
6. PIETY is the gift of feeling deep respect and reverence for God.
7. FORTITUDE is the gift of being strong and brave when faced with problems or with temptations.